ADAPTATION

GALE GEORGE

PowerKiDS
press.

NEW YORK

Published in 2017 by The Rosen Publishing Group, Inc.
29 East 21st Street, New York, NY 10010

Editor: Caitie McAneney
Book Design: Michael Flynn
Interior Layout: Tanya Dellaccio

Photo Credits: Cover Paul Nicklen/Getty Images; p. 5 4FR/Getty Images; p. 6 reptiles4all/Shutterstock.com; p. 7 (box jellyfish) Auscape/Universal Images Group/Getty Images; p. 7 (stonefish) Yann hubert/Shutterstock.com; p. 7 (puffer fish) Aries Sutanto/Shutterstock.com; p. 8 Photo 12/Universal Images Group/Getty Images; pp. 9 (sailfish), 13 Alastair Pollock Photography/Getty Images; p. 9 (cheetah) JonathanC Photography/Shutterstock.com; p. 10 Time Life Pictures/Mansell/The LIFE Picture Collection/Getty Images; p. 11 Chik_77/Shutterstock.com; p. 12 john michael evan potter/Shutterstock.com; p. 15 (main) Alexander Semenov/Getty Images; p. 15 (inset) Chanwit Polpakdee/Shutterstock.com; p. 17 (main) Pan_Da/Shutterstock.com; p. 17 (inset) Florilegius/SSPL/GettyImages; p. 18 FloridaStock/Shutterstock.com; p. 19 TravelMediaProductions/Shutterstock.com; p. 21 BUFOTO/Shutterstock.com.

Library of Congress Cataloging-in-Publication Data

Names: George, Gale.
Title: Adaptation / Gale George.
Description: New York : PowerKids Press, 2017. | Series: Spotlight on ecology and life science | Includes index.
Identifiers: ISBN 9781499425529 (pbk.) | ISBN 9781508152620 (library bound) | ISBN 9781499425536 (6 pack)
Subjects: LCSH: Adaptation (Biology)--Juvenile literature.
Classification: LCC QH546.G44 2017 | DDC 578.4--d23

Manufactured in China

CPSIA Compliance Information: Batch #BW17PK For further information contact Rosen Publishing, New York, New York at 1-800-237-9932.

CONTENTS

CHAPTER ONE

AWESOME ADAPTATIONS

There are millions of species, or kinds, of animals on this planet. From elephants to dung beetles, Earth's species are very different from one another. That's because Earth is full of many different kinds of **habitats**—from the ocean to the desert and everywhere in between.

Over time, living things adapt, or change to fit their surroundings. It can take millions of years, but in time, animals **develop** body parts and skills that set them apart from other animals. These adaptations help them live, hunt, and do their part in their **ecosystem**.

What kinds of adaptations might you find in nature? Some animals have size on their side, while others have speed. Some animals can sense things people can't. Some can give an enemy a sting or a bite full of venom, or poison. These different adaptations make the animal world **diverse**!

This Arctic wolf is white so it can blend in with its surroundings. That's an adaptation called camouflage. What other animals use camouflage?

CHAPTER TWO

PACKING POISON

There's a reason most people like to stay far away from snakes and spiders. We know that some of them have a **venomous** bite. Venomous animals deliver poison with a sting or bite, while poisonous animals are harmful if eaten or touched. Knowing that a certain animal is poisonous or venomous is enough to keep people, and predators, away from that animal. This adaptation is great for **defense** and hunting.

Vipers are some of the most venomous snakes in the world. The viper family includes rattlesnakes and cottonmouths. Vipers deliver their venom through curved, hollow teeth called fangs. Their venom disables **prey** so it's ready to be eaten. Another kind of snake called a spitting cobra can actually spray its venom at enemies.

Poison dart frogs are very tiny, colorful animals. They hold their poison in their skin. The poison in one golden poison dart frog is enough to kill 10 people.

POISON DART FROG

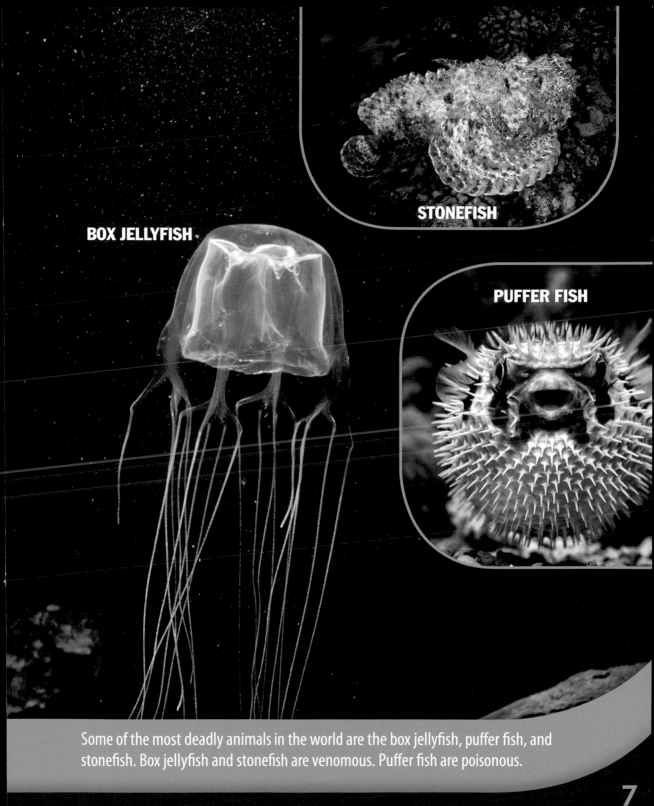

STONEFISH

BOX JELLYFISH

PUFFER FISH

Some of the most deadly animals in the world are the box jellyfish, puffer fish, and stonefish. Box jellyfish and stonefish are venomous. Puffer fish are poisonous.

CHAPTER THREE

TOP SPEED

Another great adaptation is speed. Some animals use speed to hunt, while others use it to run away from predators.

The cheetah is a famously fast animal. It can sometimes run faster than 60 miles (96.6 km) per hour. That's about as fast as a car traveling on a highway. Cheetahs don't always run, though. They save their energy for quick bursts of speed to attack their prey. Pronghorn antelopes, found in North America, are nearly as fast as cheetahs. They use their speed to run away from predators.

Peregrine falcons use their speed to swoop down and grab prey. They can dive at nearly 200 miles (321.9 km) per hour. Prey animals don't even see them coming!

Sailfish are a kind of billfish. These fish have an upper jaw that juts out and looks like a spear.

The fastest fish in the sea is the sailfish. This fish can swim at speeds of nearly 70 miles (112.7 km) per hour. The sailfish has a pointed upper jaw that's shaped like a spear and a fin on the top of its body that looks like a sail.

CHEETAH

CHAPTER FOUR

WORK AS A TEAM

Working together is a great adaptation. Some animals work together to stay safe from predators, while others come together to hunt. These animals are often good at communicating, or sharing information with one another.

Wolves are great communicators. They communicate through howls. They usually live in packs of about six to 10 members. Some wolf packs have up to 30 members. The members of the pack play different parts in hunting. A single wolf can kill a smaller animal, but a pack can take down a huge animal, such as a moose or bison.

Orcas, or killer whales, live in groups called pods. Pods are usually made up of five to 30 whales. Some pods have more than 100 whales! They communicate through **complex** calls. Orca pods work together to herd fish into one area for feeding.

ILLUSTRATION OF AN ORCA

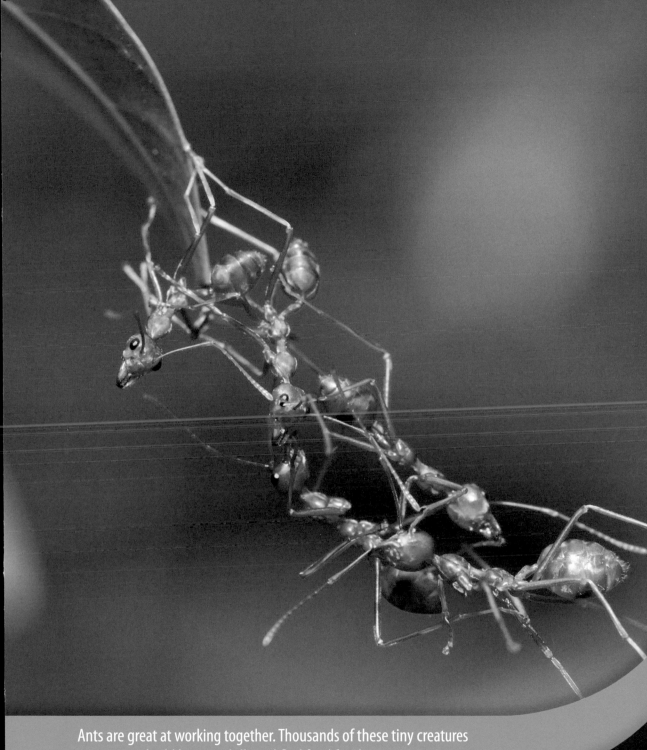

Ants are great at working together. Thousands of these tiny creatures team up to build large anthills and find food for their community.

CHAPTER FIVE

WORLD'S LARGEST

The size of an animal is another adaptation. Some animals are so big that others won't try to hunt them. Some use their size and strength to take down smaller animals.

African elephants are the largest land animals in the world. They grow up to 13 feet (4 m) tall at the shoulder. They have a long trunk that is used for smelling, calling, drinking, and grabbing food. Because of their size and the way they work together, adult elephants have no natural predators. They can live up to 70 years in the wild.

Elephants have big ears! They help the elephant hear sounds from far away. Elephants also flap their ears to communicate with one another.

Great white sharks use their huge size to hunt smaller sharks, fish, and seals. They can grow to over 20 feet (6 m) long.

The largest animal in the world is the blue whale. These whales can grow to more than 100 feet (30.5 m) long. They don't use their size to hunt, though. They would rather eat tiny ocean creatures. Blue whales are rarely attacked by other animals because of their big size. They can live for more than 100 years in the wild.

CHAPTER SIX

WAY TO GLOW!

Some animals live so deep underwater that no sunlight can reach their habitat. Life in the deep sea is cold and dark. The few creatures that live there had to adapt to these tough surroundings. Some animals, including some **bacteria**, jellyfish, and worms, can create their own light. That's an adaptation called bioluminescence.

The flashlight fish is one of the sea's bioluminescent creatures. This small fish has a photophore underneath each eye. A photophore is a body part that creates light. Flashlight fish use their light to **attract** tiny ocean creatures to eat. They also "blink" their light to confuse predators.

Some creatures glow as a defense. Blue-ringed octopuses are one of the most venomous animals in the world. When they feel scared, blue rings glow on their skin. Predators recognize this as a sign that the octopus is venomous, and they stay away.

BLUE-RINGED OCTOPUS

Most deep-sea jellyfish are bioluminescent. Some flash their light to scare predators. Others produce a glowing slime with which to coat predators.

CHAPTER SEVEN

TIME TO HIBERNATE

The winter can be a tough time for animals. When the weather gets cold, some animals lose their food sources. They have to **conserve** their energy until the winter ends. Some animals have adapted to winter by going into a deep sleep called hibernation. During hibernation, animals use very little energy and don't need to eat as much, if at all.

Bats are great at hibernation. They find safe homes inside trees, caves, and even barns or attics. Then they slip into hibernation, and their heart rate and breathing slow almost to a stop. During the winter, bats lose nearly half their weight. When they wake up, they have to hunt to make up for the weight they lost.

Ground squirrels live in many parts of North America that get very cold in the winter. They spend up to nine months hibernating underground. They sometimes wake up and move around before falling back to sleep.

BROWN LONG-EARED BAT

Bears are some of the most well-known hibernating animals. However, bears don't really hibernate. They go into a state called torpor, which is like hibernation, except the bear can wake up if necessary.

CHAPTER EIGHT

STAYING WARM

Animals must adapt to the **climate** in their habitat. Some animals live in very cold places, and they've adapted to stay warm through long winters.

Mammals that live in the Arctic often have a thick layer of blubber, or fat, under their skin. Mammals are warm-blooded animals, which means they need to keep a constant temperature in their bodies to survive. Fish don't need blubber because they're cold-blooded, which means

A thick, insulating fur coat helps polar bears stay warm. The thick layer of fat underneath their skin keeps them warm when they swim in icy water.

Penguins have a layer of blubber under their skin to help them stay warm. They sometimes huddle together for heat.

their body temperature changes to fit their surroundings. Warm-blooded Arctic animals include whales and seals. Their blubber **insulates** their body and protects the animals from the extreme cold of their habitat.

Animals that live in cold places often have thick fur, too. The musk ox is one very hairy animal, and its thick coat keeps it safe from the cold. Gray wolves have two layers of fur—the inside coat is thick and warm while the outside coat sheds water.

CHAPTER NINE

AMAZING SENSES

Humans have five basic senses: sight, hearing, touch, taste, and smell. Some animals have these senses and more! Many animals rely on supersenses to live and hunt in their habitat.

Some animals can "hear" through the ground. They pick up on vibrations, or tiny movements. Elephants can feel vibrations through their feet and trunk, which have special **sensors** in them. Snakes also hear through vibrations. Scientists think these tiny movements hit the snake's jaw as it moves along the ground. The jaw then sends the vibrations to the inner ear and then to the brain.

Sharks are master predators, and their supersenses give them an edge while hunting. Great white sharks can smell even a tiny amount of blood in the open water. Sharks also have a special body part that can pick up on the smallest movements in the water, such as the heartbeat of prey.

Vipers with special body parts called pit organs can sense heat from other animals nearby. That makes them unstoppable hunters!

CHAPTER TEN

SURVIVING IN THE WILD

From supersenses to glow-in-the-dark skin, the animal world is full of adaptations. Adaptations make animals the masters of their habitats. They're the tools that keep animals from dying out in their natural ecosystems.

Unfortunately, when habitats change, animals may not be able to change quickly enough. That's why some animals are in trouble when people change their habitats. People cut down trees for land and make buildings where meadows used to be. They drain wetlands and pollute the oceans and rivers. Forests become cities. Many animals are unable to keep up.

When an animal is at risk of dying out, it's considered threatened or endangered. Unfortunately, there are thousands of animals endangered today. Many have died out completely. It's up to humans to make sure that we keep animal habitats as wild as possible. Then these amazing, adaptable creatures can exist for years to come!

GLOSSARY

attract (uh-TRAKT) To draw something nearer.

bacteria (bak-TEER-ee-uh) Tiny creatures that can only be seen with a microscope.

climate (KLY-muht) The average weather conditions of a place over a period of time.

complex (kahm-PLEKS) Having many parts.

conserve (kuhn-SERV) To use only as much as needed.

defense (dih-FENS) A feature of a living thing that helps keep it safe.

develop (dih-VEH-luhp) To change over time.

diverse (dy-VERS) Made up of things that are different from each other.

ecosystem (EE-koh-sis-tum) A natural community of living and nonliving things.

habitat (HAA-buh-tat) The natural place where an animal or plant lives.

insulate (IHN-suh-layt) To stop heat from going into or out of something.

prey (PRAY) An animal hunted by other animals for food.

sensor (SEHN-suhr) Something that senses heat, light, motion, sound, or smells.

venomous (VEH-neh-mehs) Having a toxic bite or sting.

INDEX

PRIMARY SOURCE LIST

Page 9
Colored engraving showing a peregrine falcon. Created by Francois-Nicolas Martinet. From *Natural History of Birds, Fish, Insects, and Reptiles* by Georges-Louis Leclerc, Count of Buffon. Published in London, England. Ca. 1800.

Page 10
Engraving showing a grampus (killer whale). From *The Naturalist's Library: Mammalia: Whales, Etc.*, edited by Sir William Jardine. Published by W.H. Lizars in Edinburgh, Scotland. Ca. 1830s.

Page 17
Hand-colored engraving showing a brown long-eared bat. Created by Fournier based on an illustration by Oudart from Charles d'Orbigny's *Dictionnaire Universel d'Histoire Naturelle*. Published in Paris, France. 1849.

WEBSITES